CREATE
a STAMP

MAKE A ROAD SIGN

GO
SLO

LOOK AT
SOMETHING
UPSIDE
DOWN

"The person who makes things is a sign of hope."

—Corita Kent

www.enchantedlion.com

First edition published in 2021 by Enchanted Lion Books,
248 Creamer Street, Studio 4, Brooklyn, New York 11231

Text copyright © 2021 by Matthew Burgess
Illustrations copyright © 2021 by Kara Kramer

All works by Corita Kent copyright © 2021 to the Estate of Corita Kent/Immaculate Heart
Community/ Licensed by Artists Rights Society (ARS), New York

A CIP record is on file with the Library of Congress
ISBN 978-1-59270-316-6

Book design by Eugenia Mello

Printed in Italy by Società Editoriale Grafiche AZ
First Printing

the life & art of CORITA KENT

WORDS by
Matthew Burgess

Pictures by
Kara Kramer

Enchanted Lion Books
NEW YORK

When Frances Elizabeth Kent was a child in Hollywood, California, she discovered a hole in the hedge behind her house.

Her friend Helen lived in the house across the way,
and the two girls would slip through this leafy window
to play in the shade on sunny afternoons.

When Helen was sick with scarlet fever, they weren't allowed to play together.
But Frances had an idea: if she sat on her side of the hedge and Helen sat on the other,
they could read aloud through the passage.

Frances's parents struggled to support their six children.

Her father worked at a restaurant, a furnace company,
and later was hired to operate a jackhammer,
breaking up blacktop in blazing California heat.

Her mother started a laundry business to help make ends meet.
She'd ask her three daughters to help press collars and cuffs,
but sometimes Frances would sneak away to read, draw,
and daydream.

When Frances was in sixth grade,
Sister Noemi noticed her love of art
and offered to give her lessons.

As she painted, Frances became

a bird in the breeze
of her brush.

In high school art class, Frances and her fellow students were asked to copy classic pictures and paintings.

Frances followed the rules,

but her father, who was an artist at heart, encouraged her in a different direction:

"Why don't you do something

ORIGINAL?"

Frances pondered his question,
but years passed before she understood
what he meant or where to begin.

The summer after she graduated from high school,
Frances enrolled in drawing classes at a college nearby.

But then she made

a big
ANNOUNCEMENT

that surprised her closest friends and family.

Frances decided to become a nun.

On the day she joined the Order of the Immaculate Heart of Mary,
she processed into the chapel as Frances Elizabeth Kent,

and emerged...

maculate Heart of M

Sister Mary Corita

One of Corita's new duties was to teach
elementary schoolchildren.
At first she felt nervous, but soon
kittens, rabbits, foxes, and frogs danced
across the walls of Corita's classroom,
and bright flowers bloomed here and there.

Corita grew into a talented teacher.
She even trained young nuns who would be
teaching for the first time, taking them
on field trips and sharing ideas for bringing
creativity into the classroom.

Several years later, Sister Magdalen Mary, who ran the art department at Immaculate Heart College, asked Corita to join the faculty.

To prepare, she studied art history and took a printmaking class.
She wanted to master these techniques and share them
with her students at Immaculate Heart.

as the
COLORS
SLIPPED
THROUGH THE
SCREEN LAYER
OVER
LAYER
corita felt inspired

One afternoon, a student offered to introduce Corita
to María Sodi de Ramos Martínez, the widow of a famous Mexican muralist.

They met, and María kindly led Corita through the process.

SERIGRAPHY

ALSO KNOWN AS SILKSCREEN

1 Prepare screen

One technique: Block out where you DON'T want ink to go.

2 Place paper under screen

BL ink

Squeegee ink through screen

3

4 Lift to See Print

Repeat

again and again

again and again

again and again

again and again

and again

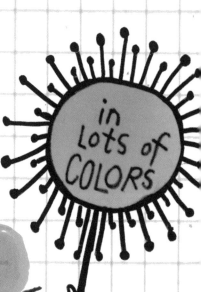

in lots of COLORS

1 Less than a year later, one of Corita's prints won FIRST PRIZE in two California competitions.

Soon, a gallery in Boston offered to show her work.

She and Sister Magdalen traveled to Massachusetts for the opening night. But first, a snowball fight!

DETOUR

2

3 The two Sisters began making yearly trips across the country, giving talks at colleges and exploring the art scene in New York City.

4 When a generous friend offered to pay their way, they embarked on a longer adventure.

They ate pastries in Paris, fed pigeons in Venice, and rode camels beside the Great Pyramid of Giza.

LA 180 miles

5 Back in Los Angeles, Corita and Magdalen were busy transforming the Immaculate Heart College art department into a lively center of art and design.

DRAW SELF PORTRAITS WITH A STICK

As an art teacher, Corita was serious about PLAY. She believed the best work is done when play and work are one.

She even created a new word:

In one assignment, Corita asked her students to cut
a small window into a piece of cardboard to make a FINDER.

LOOK

Together, they walked down Hollywood Boulevard to a gas station, car wash, and supermarket. She wanted her students to look at ordinary things until the little details came alive.

Corita explored these same approaches in her own work.

Something would catch her eye—
a billboard, a street sign, an ad in a magazine—

and she would take these words, shapes, and colors
and rearrange them into something NEW.

In her screenprint titled *song about the greatness*,
Corita borrowed the slogan for Del Monte tomato sauce.

If you look closely, you will see
she has written a Psalm inside the word "sing."

Let the ocean thunder with all its waves,
the world and all who dwell there;
the rivers clap their hands, the mountains
shout together with Joy...

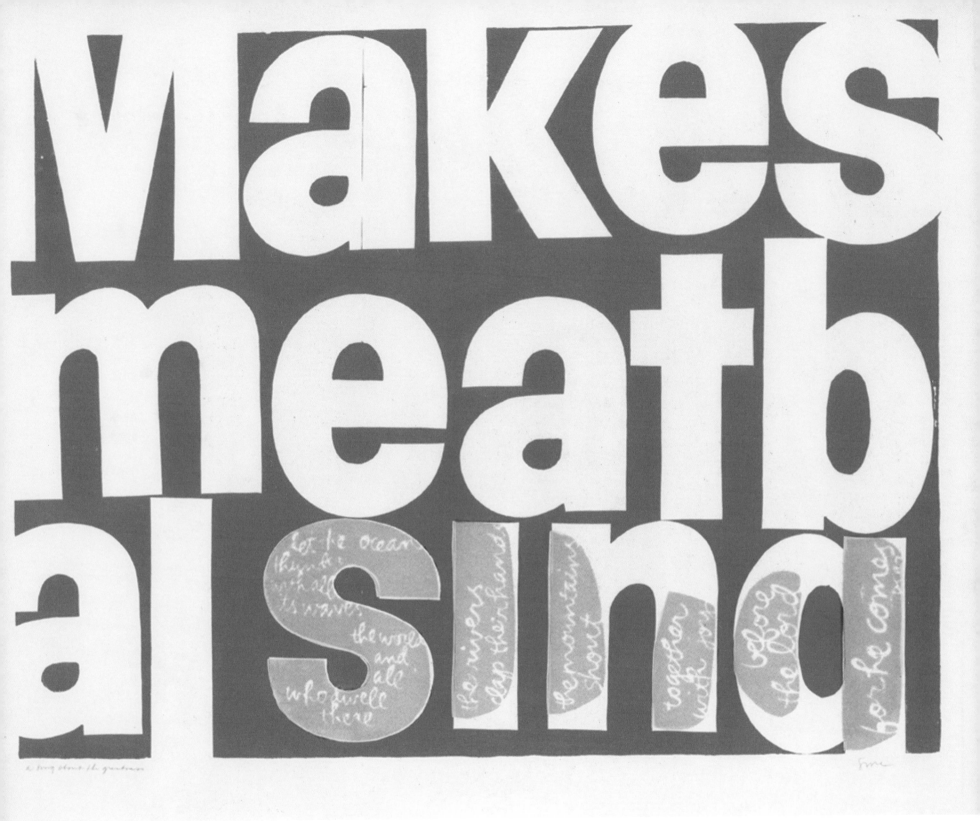

About this piece, Corita said,

"Scripture and billboards are talking to each other.
If mountains can shout and rivers clap their hands,
then meatballs can sing."

In her way, Corita invited others to see the sacred in the everyday.

At Immaculate Heart, an event called Mary's Day had been a long tradition.
Each year, students wore black and white and walked silently
across campus in straight lines.

When the college invited the art department
to do something new, Corita responded:

"Why not make it a real celebration?
If we think it's a celebration, let's make it so!"

Mary's Day exploded into a joyful picnic and parade!

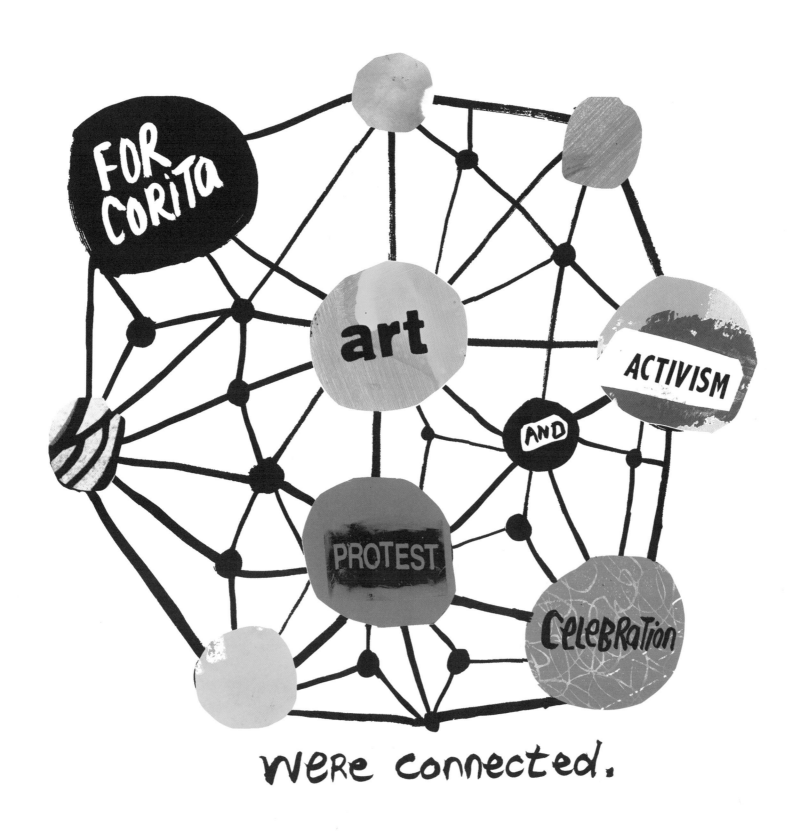

For Corita art ACTIVISM AND PROTEST CELEBRATION were connected.

She made bold prints that spoke out against injustice, poverty, and war, and she inspired others to stand up for their beliefs.

POWER UP
Stop
BOmbi
WONDE
build strong bodies 12 ways
NDARD LARGE LOAF
HOPE

In **1966**,

when Corita was 49, the *Los Angeles Times*
named her one of nine Women of the Year.

A year later, she was on the cover of Newsweek magazine!

But not everyone approved of Corita's work.
Her toughest critic by far was the Archbishop,
who complained that her art crossed the line.

For the women of Immaculate Heart,
the moment had arrived for the Church
to adapt to the changing times.

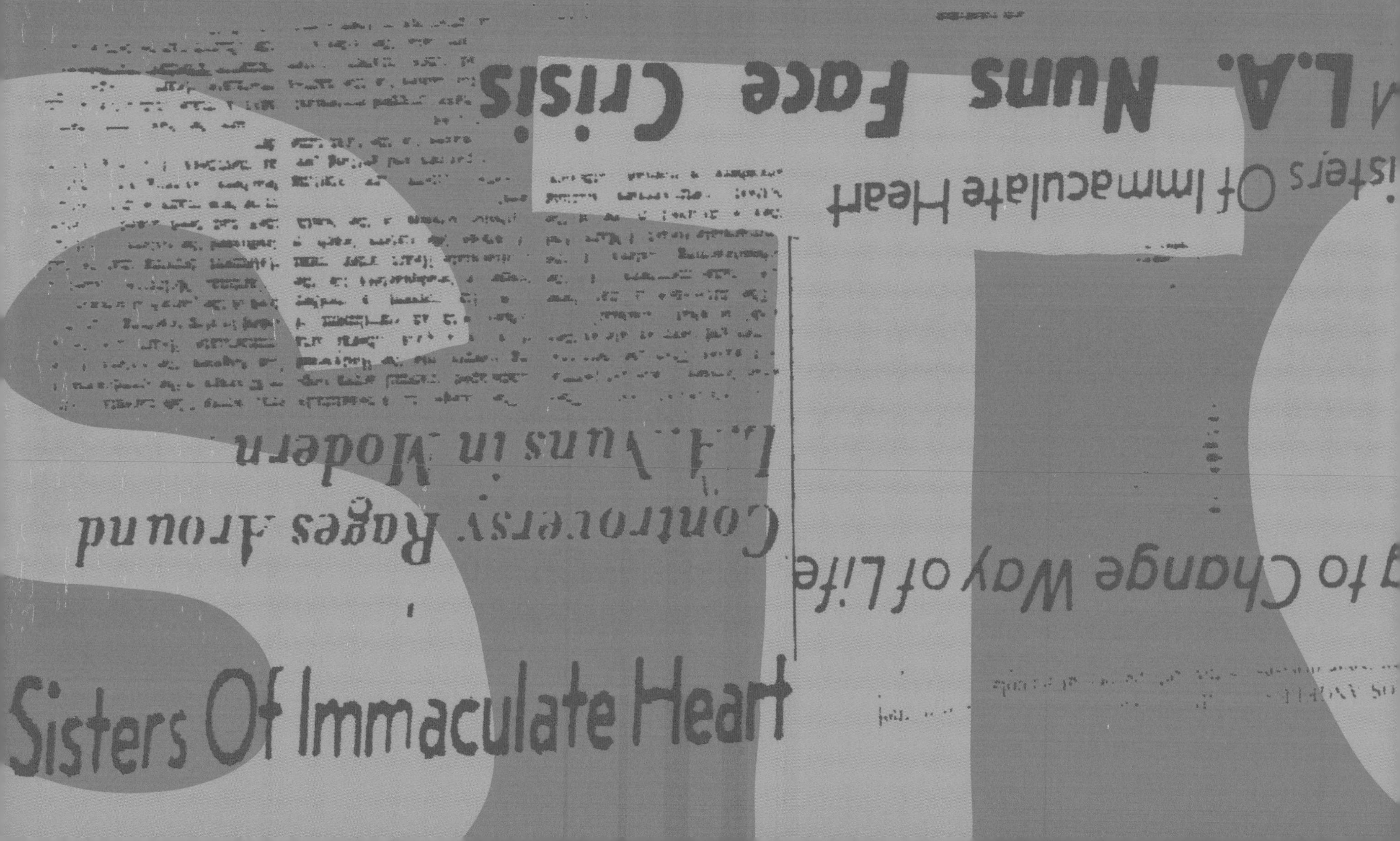

L.A. Nuns Face Crisis

isters Of Immaculate Heart

L.A. Nuns in Modern

Controversy Rages Around

to Change Way of Life

Sisters Of Immaculate Heart

When the sisters pushed for more reforms,
the Archbishop crushed their requests.

Corita needed a break.

She was given a six-month leave.
For the first time in years, she was able
to come and go as she pleased.

And before her sabbatical was over,
Corita made an announcement that again
surprised her closest friends and family.

At age 50, Corita asked to be released from her vows.

She had been a teacher and a Sister of the Immaculate Heart
for over thirty years, and she was ready for a new adventure.

Corita moved to Boston and continued to create new work.

The Boston Gas Company asked her to paint
a gigantic tank along the expressway.

It was the

BIGGEST

rainbow of Corita's artistic career...

The largest copyrighted work of art in the world!

Years later, her smallest rainbow appeared
when the United States Postal Service commissioned
Corita to design a stamp. It reached people
all over the world—selling over 700 million!

For Corita, the rainbow was a symbol of the love, hope, and kindness that unite people across the globe, regardless of their differences.

Toward the end of her life, Corita
liked to drive with a friend to the beach
or to a field with a river running through it.

Poised with her watercolors under the open sky,
she would look out

AND FEEL the JOY of BECOMING....

a
Bird
in the
BReeze
of her
BRUSH

Namaste

I greet
the light
in you

ed 500

Corita

Chronology

1918
Frances Elizabeth Kent is born on November 20, 1918, in Fort Dodge, Iowa.

1920–24
The Kent family moves to Hollywood, California. Frances attends the nearby Blessed Sacrament School for first grade.

1929–30
When Frances is in sixth grade, her teacher, Sister Noemi Cruz, IHM, recognizes her talent and offers to give her art lessons after school. Notably, Sister Noemi had been taking classes at UCLA at a time when enrollment among women was slim, and she shared her knowledge and love of art with her young student. Corita later recalls this early support from Order of the Immaculate Heart of Mary as a formative experience in her development as an artist.

1936
Frances graduates from Los Angeles Catholic Girls' High School. She surprises her friends and family by announcing that she will join the Order of the Immaculate Heart of Mary. Upon entering the convent, Frances becomes Sister Mary Corita.

1941
While teaching elementary school, Corita completes her college degree at Immaculate Heart College (IHC).

1944–47
Corita is assigned to teach at the Blessed Heart School in Vancouver, British Columbia, and she teaches at three different schools over the course of those years.

1947
Sister Magdalen Mary Martin asks Corita to join the art department faculty at Immaculate Heart College. She begins taking graduate classes in art history at University of Southern California.

1951
Corita earns her master's degree from USC and becomes fascinated with silkscreen printing. She credits María Sodi de Ramos Martínez for teaching her about the silkscreen process.

1952
Corita's print, *the lord is with thee*, wins first prize in two California art competitions.

1954
Corita has an exhibition at the Botolph Gallery in Boston. Her reputation as a teacher and artist grows, and she begins to take yearly trips across the country with Sister Magdalen Mary Martin.

1959
A student in one of the evening classes at Immaculate Heart College offers to fund a three-month tour of Spain, Italy, France, Egypt, and Turkey for Corita and Sister Magdalen Mary.

1962
Corita takes her students to see Andy Warhol's *Campbell's Soup Can* paintings at the Ferus Gallery. In October, Pope John XXIII convenes Vatican II, a call for the Catholic Church to update its practices to suit the changing, modern world.

1964
IHC president Sister Mary William [Helen Kelley] invites Corita and the Art Department to plan the annual Mary's Day celebration. Corita becomes chair of the IHC Art Department. In response to President Johnson's "War on Poverty," she collaborates on a Mary's Day Celebration with the motto "Food for Peace."

1966
At age 49, Corita is named one of the *Los Angeles Times's* nine Women of the Year. Following the message of Vatican II, Immaculate Heart members take concrete steps to adapt to the changing world, but the Archdiocese, led by Cardinal MacIntyre, pushes back against their reforms.

1967
Corita's book, *Footnotes and Headlines: A Play-Pray Book*, is published. In December, she is featured on the cover of the Christmas issue of *Newsweek* magazine.

fig 1 *

fig 2 *

1968

Following a sabbatical in Cape Cod, Massachusetts, Corita receives dispensation from her vows and begins a new chapter of her life in Boston. She maintains close ties to the Immaculate Heart Community and Los Angeles throughout her life.

1970

Damn Everything But The Circus is published. The title comes from a poem by E. E. Cummings.

1971

Corita receives a major commission from Boston Gas to design a 140-foot tank visible from the Southeast Expressway. Corita's artwork, *The Rainbow Swash*, becomes the largest copyrighted artwork in the world.

1974

Corita is diagnosed with cancer.

1985

Love Stamp is issued by the United States Postal Service. It becomes one of the bestselling stamps of all time.

1986

Corita dies in Watertown, Massachusetts, at age 67. In a letter to friends and family, she writes: "I feel this new life is just a next step and that I will still be knowing and caring for all of you forever."

Fig. 1. Immaculate Heart College Mary's Day, 1964.
Fig. 2. Corita in classroom, ca. 1964.

Author's Note

In the suburban Southern California of my childhood, Corita Kent was a well-known artist. Her prints were displayed in the homes of family friends, and her iconic *Love Stamp* made its debut on an episode of *The Love Boat* when I was eleven years old. As a child, I didn't know Corita by name, but her work was a part of the visual culture of the time—perhaps especially among Catholic families who were excited about Vatican II.

I went to Catholic schools for twelve years just south of Cardinal McIntyre's diocese in Los Angeles. I remember the old monsignor with the bellowing voice who said the morning Mass in Latin. I also remember young Sister Cheryl grabbing her guitar and leading us in songs. In this childlike way, I witnessed the tension in the church between those who pushed for reforms and the more conservative forces which resisted. I was definitely more drawn to rainbows and singalongs than the Latin Mass!

Many years later, when my first picture book biography, *Enormous Smallness: A Story of E. E. Cummings* was about to publish, I relayed that news to Eva Payne, my cousin's partner, who was assisting in the preparations for a Corita Kent retrospective at Harvard Art Museum. "Corita loved Cummings," she said. "She quoted lines of his poetry in her prints." Down the rabbit hole I happily tumbled, and in looking at Corita's work online, I found it at once familiar and revelatory. The vivid colors and rainbow swashes pulsed in memory. The more I learned about Corita's life, art, and teaching, the more excited I became about sharing her story with young people.

Like Keith Haring, another one of my artistic heroes, Corita believed that art is for everyone. This is one of the reasons she connected so strongly with silkscreen printing; she could make many copies of the same serigraph and thereby share it more widely. Corita also believed that every person possesses creative potential, and as a teacher myself, I wholeheartedly agree. With her students, she often referred to the Balinese saying "We have no art. We do everything as well as we can" as a way to emphasize process over product and attention over perfection. Corita consistently invited everyone into the circle—and she did this within the rigid hierarchy of the Catholic church during the social and political upheaval of the 1960s and 70s.

While Corita was developing as an artist, the country was grappling with injustice, social division, and the ongoing threat of nuclear war. People were fearful about the future. Like many of her sisters in the Immaculate Heart Community, Corita did not hide from the challenges of her time. She felt the call to act, and she insisted that despair wasn't an option. Her close friend Daniel Berrigan, the poet, peace activist, and Jesuit priest, put it this way: "We couldn't just lose [ourselves] in the harsh realities of war and survival, but we had to say 'Yes' that was a little louder than 'No.'" This form of social action—rooted in joy—is something that Corita's life and art continue to teach us.

In her essay titled 'Art and Beauty in the Life of the Sister', Corita wrote: 'Poets and artists—makers—look long and lovingly at commonplace things, rearrange them and put their rearrangements where others can notice them too.' Throughout her body of work, Corita invites us to discover the spark of spirit within the most ordinary things. "Makes meatballs sing" was simply a slogan for Del Monte tomato sauce until Corita lifted it from the label and transformed it in her bold print. In her beautiful way, Corita avoided preachiness and direct statement. She wanted the viewer to reflect, to wonder, to play with the meaning of the metaphor. I think Corita might be hinting that we are the meatballs, and she is calling us to sing.

—Matthew Burgess

Illustrator's Note

I am standing on a street corner in NYC and for some reason pause to check my email. What I read gives me chills: Wow...What!

It's a note from Claudia at Enchanted Lion asking me if I would be interested in illustrating a book about this amazing woman from the 60s who was a pop artist and a nun, named Corita Kent. Just a week prior, I had noticed the Corita Art Center was having a competition to celebrate her 100th birthday and wanted to submit a collage. And now this, a whole book, about an artist to whom I had been drawn as if by intuition over the past decade. I don't remember the first time I saw one of Corita's prints, but her love for color, use of words, collage, and bold techniques—everything resonated so strongly with me, I could never get enough of it.

So, of course, I said "YES!" to this project. Working on *Make Meatballs Sing* has given me time to learn more about Corita's life as a nun, artist, activist, and teacher, and to look closely at her vibrant artwork. I also picked up the book *Learning by Heart*, which I now often flip open to any page. In it, Corita shares assignments to get the maker in you making, exploring, observing, discovering new connections, and using materials in a fun way—like drawing the alphabet with a chopstick.

I'm deeply grateful for this experience to collaborate with Claudia and Matthew, and I like to think Corita, too, who seemed to be in the very air around me, especially in the beginning of this process. I remember walking my dog one day in Brooklyn and stopping because right there at my feet was a bag of popcorn, with the words "fresh and hot," printed in red, and a bird close by eating the crumbs. It felt like Corita was winking at me, reminding me to "Go Slow," and notice the WONDER happening right before my eyes.

Within the pages of this book, you can find the "fresh and hot" popcorn bag.

—Kara Kramer

Dressed for a celebration

Matthew Burgess

Matthew Burgess is a full-time professor at Brooklyn College and a part-time teaching artist in New York City public schools. He was fascinated by the lives of saints as a child, and now he loves sharing the stories of his artistic heroes with young readers. Matthew is also the author of *Enormous Smallness: A Story of E. E. Cummings* and *Drawing on Walls: A Story of Keith Haring.* He lives with his husband in Brooklyn and Berlin.

Taking in small bits of the world

Kara Kramer

Kara Kramer is a mixed-media artist and illustrator who loves to PLORK with all mediums. She has taught creative art workshops for both children and adults. Ever since she was little, her favorite hours are spent moving her hands to make something new. She lives in Brooklyn, New York with her family.

fig 3 *

Acknowledgements

First and foremost, we would like to thank Nellie Scott and the entire community at the Corita Art Center for their generous collaboration and support. Matthew also would like to thank Eva Payne, Anne Crouchley, Liz Greenhill, Ray Smith, Reza Memari, Marija Stojnic, and the Sacatar Foundation. The first draft of the manuscript was written during a residency at Instituto Sacatar on the island of Itaparica in Bahia, Brazil.

Fig. 3. Corita in classroom, ca. 1968.

For more information about Corita, including wonderful photos of her and her artwork, please visit the Corita Art Center at www.corita.org.

Quotation Sources

"The person who makes things is a sign of hope." * "The Nun: A Joyous Revolution." *Newsweek,* December 25, 1967.

"Why don't you do something original?" * As recalled by Corita in an interview with Bernard Galm. UCLA Library Center for Oral History Research, April 1976.

"Consider everything an experiment." "Nothing is a mistake. There's no win and no fail. There's only make." * From the "Immaculate Heart College Art Department Rules."

"Pretend you are a microscope." "New ideas are bursting all around and all this comes into you and is changed by you." "Doing and making are acts of hope and as that hope grows, we stop feeling overwhelmed by the troubles of the world. We remember that we— as individuals and groups—can do something about those troubles." * Corita Kent and Jan Steward. *Learning By Heart: Teachings to Free the Creative Spirit.* New York: Bantam Books, 1992.

"Scripture and billboards are talking to each other. If mountains can shout and rivers clap their hands, then meatballs can sing." * Corita Kent. "Choose Life or Assign a Sign or Begin a Conversation," *Living Light 3*, No. 1. Spring 1966.

"Poets and artists—makers—look long and lovingly at commonplace things, rearrange them and put their rearrangements where others can notice them too." Corita Kent. "Art and Beauty in the Life of a Sister." In *The Changing Sister*, edited by Sister Charles Borromeo Muckenhirn. Notre Dame, Indiana: Fides Publishers, 1965.

"Why not make it a real celebration? If we think it's a celebration, let's make it so!" (Corita)
"We couldn't just lose [ourselves] in the harsh realities of war and survival, but we had to say 'Yes' that was a little louder than 'No.'" (Daniel Berrigan) * *Someday is Now: The Art of Corita Kent.* Eds. Ian Berry and Michael Duncan. Saratoga Springs, N.Y.: Frances Tang Teaching Museum and Art Gallery at Skidmore College; Munich: DelMonico Books/Prestel, 2013.

"Doing and Making
are Acts of Hope
and as that
Hope GROWS
we stop feeling
overwhelmed by
the troubles of the
World. We Remember
that we as individuals
and Groups can
Do something
about these troubles."
— corita